SINFUL CINEMA SERIES

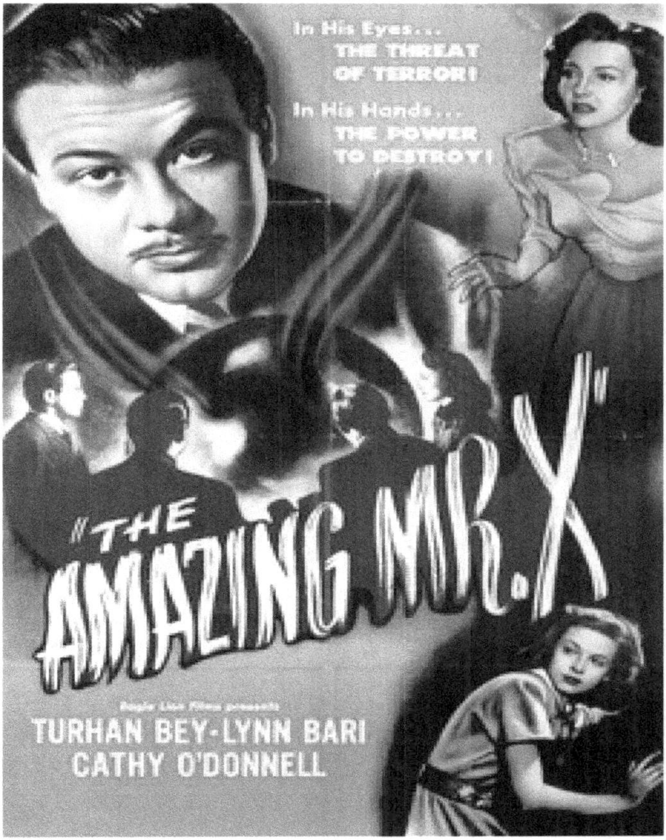

SINFUL CINEMA SERIES

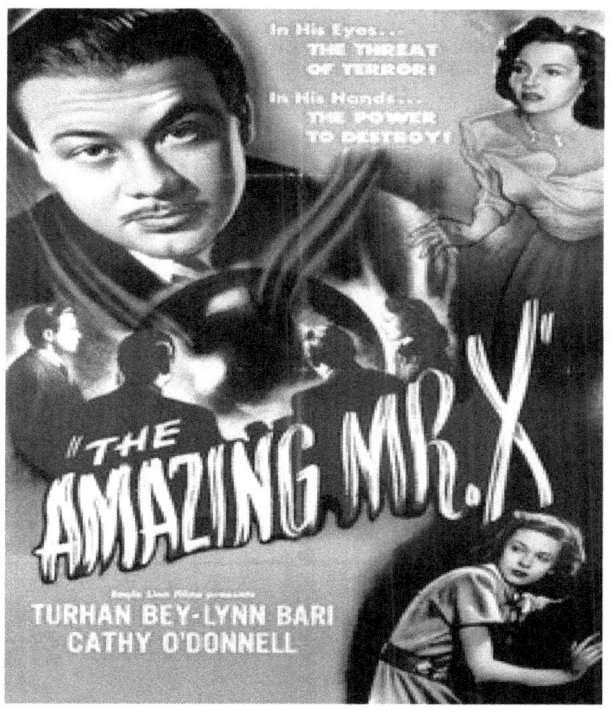

Doug Brunell

SINFUL CINEMA SERIES: THE AMAZING MR. X

by

Doug Brunell

©2020 Doug Brunell

Chaotic Words

Front and back cover illustration: film poster

This book is licensed for your personal enjoyment only. Any photos not credited in this book are utilized under Fair Use and are merely to illustrate a point. As with any film critique, the opinions I state are not to be taken as fact. They are merely opinions. Your enjoyment of the film at hand may vary.

ACKNOWLEDGEMENTS

This book could not have been done without you, the readers. I would have never made it to a fifth volume without the positive feedback from you fine people who have read the other books in this series. Perhaps the best response I get is, "Your book made me want to watch the movie again." Then there are some people who want to see the film covered for the first time after merely reading the book's blurb. I take that as a compliment in the highest form, and I thank you.

THE CROW

The fifth volume is here, and it covers a film unlike anything featured in the first four volumes of this series. This book delves into *The Amazing Mr. X,* which is a 1948 *noir* film disguised as a horror flick. Like the films in the first four books, this one was chosen at random, and it was one I had never seen prior to watching it for this book.

Before dismissing this film as a black and white snorefest, which is something today's audiences are far too quick to do with older movies, I suggest you read my take on it. If you think it sounds interesting, I advise you to watch it for yourself. It is a public domain film, so it should be easy to find (as I write this there are several different posts of it on YouTube, all of various qualities). If you have seen it, I would be curious to hear your take on it. Feel free to share your thoughts about it on the Sinful Cinema Facebook page.

And now the big question: Why title this introduction the way I did? That you will soon learn. In the meantime, onto our feature presentation . . .

THE AMAZING MR. X

The black and white film opens with a coastal scene shot from high above. A woman is walking along the shore as waves break to her right.

The scene shifts to a shot of a mansion on a cliff above the ocean. Christine (Lynn Bari) stands on the balcony of the mansion looking down at the beach and ocean below. Behind her, from inside the room, a shadow appears on the wall. It appears to be the shadow of a man holding a gun. The shadow is inching its way to the open door of the balcony, and then it shifts into a better perspective. Instead of a man with a gun, it is really Christine's sister, Janet (Cathy O'Donnell), holding a hairbrush.

Christine tells her sister that she thought she heard a man's voice outside calling her name. She says it sounded like Paul (Donald Curtis), but that seems impossible because he has been dead for two years.

Christine is getting ready to go on a date with a man named Martin (Richard Carlson) despite that she could never love another man like she loved Paul. Christine is going on this date dressed in black and wearing her wedding ring, much to Janet's surprise. Janet convinces her sister to change into a white dress instead. Surprisingly, both Janet and Christine think Martin may propose on this date. Janet also takes the time to remind Christine that she has a date of her own, but she forgot the man's name.

Martin, who is a lawyer, calls Christine to tell her he may be late for the date because someone came into the office at the last minute. Christine tells him that she will walk along the beach to his house. He warns her against doing that because it is not safe. Before Christine leaves the mansion, her maid (Virginia Gregg) has some parting words.

Christine, now in the white dress, walks along the beach. She hears a male voice gurgling out her name. She then passes by a small wooden boat on the shore. The name "Paul" is painted on its side. A crow on a branch calls at her. Christine looks back at the crow and then runs right into a man smoking a pipe.

This mysterious, eloquent, soft-spoken man tells Christine that he saw that her husband was dead, his car was in flames, and she was to marry a new man. The stranger's name is Alexis (Turhan Bey), and he is a "psychic consultant." He hands her his business card and tells her that they are alike in that they are both free spirits. He says they are not like Martin. Christine is surprised that Alexis knows Martin's name and mannerisms along with all the other things he has revealed.

Martin comes walking along the beach calling for Christine. Alexis, who had told her that they will not meet again, disappears when she looks away toward Martin's voice. Martin finds Christine, and she says she wants to cancel their date because she is upset. Martin understands and walks her back to her house. Once there she goes upstairs to fix her dress, which got torn, as Martin pours them drinks. When she comes back downstairs they kiss and Martin leads her to the sofa and then puts on music.

Christine thinks the music is familiar but tells Martin that she does not own the record he is playing. She tells him that it is Paul's favorite prelude that he used to play on the piano.

Martin begs her to forget Paul, something Christine agrees she should do. Martin tells her that if he cannot make her forget Paul, maybe she should find someone who can. They tease each other a bit more, and he proposes, sliding a ring onto her finger. A painting of Paul sitting at a piano is between them as they move to kiss. Christine looks at the ominous painting.

Later that night Christine is asleep. She has replaced the photo of Paul by her bed with one of Martin. Next to that on her nightstand are the flowers Martin brought her and her engagement ring. The door to her balcony opens of its own accord and a male voice asks Christine to race to the beach.

Christine responds in her sleep, but then wakes up and goes to the balcony to look out at the ocean. A breeze causes Martin's photo to blow over and break. Christine shuts the balcony door and walks to the photo. Oddly enough, the flowers are dead and there is a different ring on the nightstand. The photo of Martin has also been replaced with Paul's photo. Then an apparition of Christine's wedding dress appears in the closet!

The apparition of the dress follows Christine throughout the room as she tries to evade it. She screams as she is cornered by it, and Janet comes running to her aid.

Unfortunately, the door to Christine's room is locked, so Janet is unable to enter and save her sister. Then the door mysteriously unlocks and Janet rushes into the room to find Christine on the floor. Janet helps her to her feet as Christine explains what happened. Janet thinks it was a dream. On the nightstand the engagement ring and Martin's picture have returned, and the flowers are fresh once again. Janet says the wedding dress was really Christine's bathrobe, which is hanging on the door to the closet. Christine says she thinks Paul does not want her to marry Martin. Janet tells her sister she should talk to an analyst, but Christine fears one would only think she is losing her mind. She would rather talk to Alexis because she thinks he would understand.

Janet sees Christine to bed and gets her a glass of water. Christine, still shaken by the incident, asks Janet to share the bed for the night.

Later, Christine, with Alexis' business card in hand, pays the man a visit. The front door of his large house opens by itself and closes behind her once she enters. There is a crow on a perch in the house. A door opens off to the side of the room, and the crow flies through the opening. Christine follows it to find Alexis smoking a cigarette in the room.

Alexis describes to Christine the people who normally come to see him for his services. He turns off the lights in the room, bathing them in shadow as they sit at a table with a small amount of sunlight streaming into the room behind them. A crystal ball lights up in the middle of the table as Alexis announces that he thinks Christine is a believer. Alexis also tells her that Paul's presence is so strong that it may be dangerous to her. He then asks her to have the courage to explore.

A few weeks seem to pass, and Janet and Martin spy on Christine as she goes to visit Alexis again. They hire Hoffman (Harry Mendoza), a detective, to investigate Alexis. Hoffman tells them that he believes spiritual mediums are nothing but grifters. He reveals that he used to be a magician himself. He does a trick where playing cards come out of his mouth, which seems to scare Janet.

Hoffman happens to have a file on Alexis from a prior investigation. Hoffman reveals that Alexis served time in jail. He used a different name and swindled a rich lady out of her money. Janet uses that information to come up with a plan to send someone Alexis does not know to see him in order to get his fingerprints.

Later, at Alexis' house, the spiritualist uses a hidden video monitor to witness Janet at his front door, which opens on its own as it did for her sister weeks earlier.

Janet, posing as Mrs. Charles Harper, enters the room and sees a pad of paper on a table in front of a mirror. Written instructions state that she is supposed to write her question on the paper. She does so, tears the sheet of paper from the pad, and hides it. Alexis, on the other side of the mirror, watches her apply lipstick. He also uses a hidden sliding tray to access the pad of paper she used so that he can see the imprint of her question on it.

Alexis makes his presence known and surprises Janet by stating that he knows her question is false. Then he, seemingly unsurprised by her fake identity, reveals that he knows she is worried about her older, though less mature sister. Janet is starting to become convinced of his powers, and they share cigarettes. Alexis willingly puts his fingerprints on a cigarette case as the detective and Martin wait outside. Janet, now feeling guilty of trying to trick the man, tells Alexis that she hopes she has not done anything illegal in trying to help her sister. He gives Janet the cigarette case and tells her to do what she thinks is best.

Janet leaves the house and walks down the street as Martin pulls up in his car beside her. She tells Martin that she got the fingerprints but erased them because Alexis is not the type of man Martin believes him to be.

Alexis has a lover named Emily, who it is revealed has been disguising herself as Christine's maid. She comes home to him and they begin talking of their scams. A rich female visitor arrives, and Alexis quickly dons a turban. The visitor writes down her question in front of the mirror, and a new scam begins.

At Christine's house, Janet begs her sister not to see Alexis again. Janet lets it slip that she has talked to the man, and it seems like she is enamored with him. Christine leaves the house to drive to Alexis'. Janet follows her while Alexis watches them arrive at his house via the monitor.

When the two women enter the house, Alexis tells them that he is about to do a séance. At his request, Janet ties his wrists behind his back and Christine locks him in a cabinet and turns out the lights. The sisters then sit at the table with a crystal ball on it and hold hands.

Soon a ghostly hand appears out of the darkness near them, and then a ghostly vision of their father's face appears. They also feel a chilly breeze.

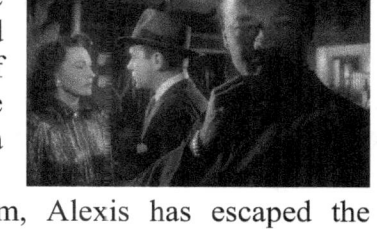

Unbeknownst to them, Alexis has escaped the cabinet and is behind these apparitions, including when the ladies hear piano music playing and see ghostly hands at the keys.

Meanwhile, Martin and Hoffman have arrived outside Alexis' house.

Back inside the house, Alexis secretly dons a mask of Paul's face and appears before the women. Martin and Hoffman break into the house at just this moment, interrupting the séance. Surprisingly, Alexis manages to disappear and is found by the group. He happens to be back in the cabinet with his wrists retied.

Martin admits to investigating Paul and reveals that Paul was scamming Christine and Paul's first wife died. Detective Hoffman examines the cabinet and declares that he wants another séance.

They all sit at the table for the séance, and Alexis says that it will not work due to the anger in the room. Alexis tries to get up from the table, but Martin and the detective will not let him. Piano music begins playing, seeming to surprise Alexis. Paul's voice then calls out to Christine and he appears in a doorway.

Alexis tries to stop the men from chasing Paul, but they break from his grip and go after him. Paul has disappeared, however. Alexis announces that the séance has left him strained and excuses himself. Janet takes Christine home. Once alone, Alexis pours himself a drink. He is confused by what has occurred. That is when Paul appears behind him.

Paul is not a spirit but is in fact still alive. He claims to be only "legally" dead, and he has been keeping an eye on Alexis ever since Christine started coming to the mystic. He takes Alexis' drink from him and tells him he has plans for the two of them to get money from Christine. Alexis realizes that Paul cannot return alive to Christine due to the body found in the car that was believed to be Paul's.

Paul starts to play the piano. He is playing a tune that he played for his first wife. Both men realize they are in a precarious position. If either man tells the truth about the other, they risk being exposed as criminals. Paul wants Alexis to marry Janet in order to get the ladies' estate. Paul states he will "take care" of Christine. Paul leaves the room, but not before asking Alexis to have the piano tuned.

Back at Christine's mansion, Emily and Alexis convince Christine to drink some milk, which she does not realize has been drugged. Christine says she keeps hearing Paul's spirit calling to her. She wants to break off contact with that spirit, but Alexis insists that they do not do that. Christine decides she wants to do a séance, but Alexis tells her he cannot conduct one until he is more familiar with his surroundings. Janet offers to walk outside with him and show him around the grounds.

The two go down to the beach. Paul is hiding outside, and Alexis nods his head as a signal to the man. Janet reveals to Alexis that she believes she also has the power to contact spirits and rests her head on his shoulder.

Back in the mansion, the drugged milk has taken effect and Christine sleeps.

Still on the beach, Janet and Alexis talk about Christine and how she will always belong to Paul. Janet professes loving Alexis and they kiss. The camera cuts to the ocean's waves.

Christine awakens to the sound of the piano playing. She is still groggy from the drugged milk. To her surprise, she sees Paul at the piano. He tells her he has come for her and then walks out onto the balcony. He starts to lead her to the beach, but Christine is frightened. He offers to race her there and starts to run off. Christine follows him, but slips down the side of the cliff. Janet and Alexis run to her and reach her before she can fall all the way down to the beach. She is unharmed.

Martin arrives at the mansion and finds Alexis there with his crow on his shoulder. The staff is all gone, and Martin asks Janet where he can find Christine. Janet tells him all that has transpired.

Christine, who has retired to her room, hears Paul's voice. Paul is in another room speaking through a microphone connected to a hidden speaker. Christine, unaware of how she is being tricked, walks to the balcony.

Janet and Martin hear a noise upstairs. They think Christine has fallen to her death, but she was getting aspirin. Martin advises her to go to a hospital, but she kicks Martin out of her home instead.

Alexis and Paul talk. Paul admits to Alexis that he killed his first wife after she backed out of a settlement and would do the same to Alexis if he backs out of their deal.

Paul puts on a record that Janet hears over a hidden speaker. Unfortunately for Paul, she also hears him talking. When the record gets stuck in place, Janet becomes suspicious and finds one of the hidden 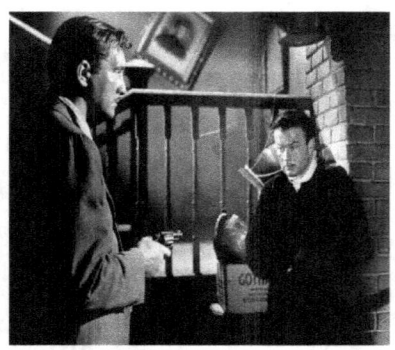 speakers. She rushes to investigate and finds Alexis, who warns her to leave. She then sees Paul, who pulls out a gun. Alexis intervenes and stops the shooting. Janet flees as a fight breaks out between Paul and

Alexis. Janet tries to place a call to Martin, but Paul rips out the phone line.

Janet runs upstairs to wake Christine. Paul arrives at Christine's room and draws his gun one more time to finish the job. Alexis, meanwhile, uses an axe to cut the house's electricity, plunging them into near darkness. Alexis uses the microphone to speak over the speaker to Paul (despite the lack of electricity). He tells Paul that he forgot about Alexis' power to raise the dead. Paul locks the girls in the room and goes to confront Alexis, who has now donned black garb to blend into the darkness. Paul shoots randomly, and tells Alexis that if he were a ghost, bullets would not hurt him. Alexis informs Paul he is out of bullets just as the police arrive. Paul states he has one bullet left, which he uses to fire at the police. The police return fire and shoot Paul.

Alexis has been shot as well, though, and Janet comforts him. His crow is watching nearby. Alexis asks Janet to open the window. When she does so, Alexis tells the crow to fly away as he is no longer needed.

The crow exits the open window.

The Amazing Mr. X (1948, 78 minutes) starts with a major strike against it. That strike is in the form of its title. It is a title which conjures just about every type of movie other than what this one is, and that was most likely true for audiences when it was originally released. If one were going to attend a film in 1948, this perhaps sounded like an interesting sci-fi one, and it makes one wonder if it would have been better off under its other title, *The Spiritualist*.

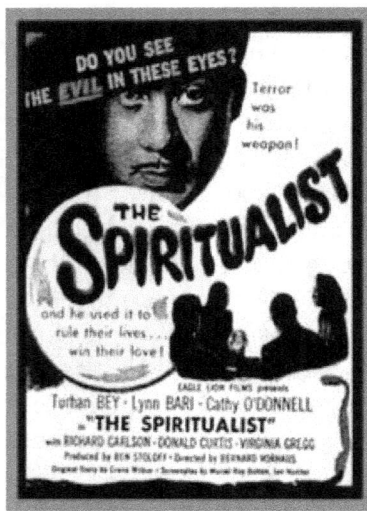

Incidentally, one cannot help but wonder if the title the movie is more widely known under was in any way influenced by Emanuel Julius' short fictional piece titled *The Strange Mr. X* that appeared in volume one, issue 16 of the San Francisco anarchist newspaper *The Blast*.

That story, which was published in the paper's July 15, 1916 issue, features an evasive stranger with a "soft voice" who had a "keen sense of appreciation" and a "spiritual calm." Mr. X was also described as "Christ-like" with a "majestic serenity" about him. In many ways, this mirrors audiences' first reactions to Alexis, with mystical powers replacing the "Christ-like" demeanor. Alexis, of course, is a scam artist who has a turn of heart at the end, while the Mr. X of Julius' story goes out of his way to value every life he encounters (including that of an ant), but in the end is revealed to be the state executioner.

The Strange Mr. X is all about how appearances can fool people, which is also a key component of

The Amazing Mr. X, despite its science-fiction-like title.

Director Bernard Vorhaus' film is, of course, not a sci-fi film, but a *noir* crime drama with horror movie trappings. What makes it interesting is that these supernatural horror movie tropes (disembodied voices, spirits, misplaced items, etc.) are first utilized against both the characters in the film *and* the audience. Later, as the plot progresses, the audience is let in on the scheme at roughly the same time as the film's ancillary protagonists. It is a subtle, yet effective narrative shift that keeps the audience's interest. Unfortunately, the outcome is far from interesting and is instead the norm for these types of films.

Just about everything in *The Amazing Mr. X*, besides the title, works on some level. With few exceptions, however, that is all it does – simply works. It is a story that has been told before populated with characters we all know, but it is done in a way that does not insult the audience's intelligence … too much. The term "utilitarian" comes to mind when describing the film, but while it is crafted in such a way, there are also some great touches that show some real artistry at work. Taken alone, this film is worth its running time if one does not expect too much from it, and that lack of expectation must start with the story.

The movie's plot is nothing out of the ordinary when it comes to a *noir* film genre with the exception of the fake supernatural element in its beginnings.

That itself is a nice touch that sets this movie apart from others, especially because it was handled so deftly. The rest of the story, however, which is basically that of con men trying to trick wealthy women out of their money, was nothing new even in 1948. As we will learn later, however, that time period did let this film be seen differently than modern audiences see it now.

Taken on its own, without attaching audience expectations to it, one can easily determine that though the story is cliché in many ways, it is also solidly told. The audience is kept in the dark when it needs to be, enlightened at the right times, and is able to focus on the narrative instead of the standard tropes. Vorhaus created a film that does not play the audience for fools and actually treats its subject matter seriously, which is the only way a film attempting to do what is attempted here could feasibly work. If too much emphasis was given to one facet over another, or if one aspect of the story was played for a joke, the entire movie would have crumbled like a house of marked cards. It is a tightrope that Vorhaus and the actors walk, but they navigate the pitfalls of the tale quite well, and part of that is contributable to the characters and the actors who played them.

It is a rare thing when not a single character is taken for granted by a film. One can easily say some characters were not explored enough, or seemed to be throwaways, but there were not many of those, and one could just as easily argue that each character actually served their role quite well, even if that role was not totally spelled out at first. The main roles, however, are the real focus of the story and should have been. Alexis, Christine, Janet, and Paul each represent a different type of personality with all their strengths and weaknesses. Martin, however, serves a different purpose, which will be delved into shortly.

Alexis is the main character of the story. He is, after all, the title character, and that title is the first bit of misdirection that occurs. It leads viewers to believe that not only is Alexis "amazing," but that he is also the protagonist from the start, though a bit of an unsettling one.

The opening shot looking down on the beach sets up Alexis' introduction quite well. At first it appears to be a calm scene with no supernatural tinge to it. The second time we see the same scene a short while later in the film it is now filled with dread, as we know Christine should not be running along the beach. Then we meet Alexis' crow, which is representative of different things to different cultures. Many cultures, due to its black color and the fact that it dined on corpses, related the crow to death. Some Native American tribes believe it to be a trickster or a missionary. Here it is so out of place on the beach that it is unsettling. Then Alexis appears.

Seeing Alexis on the beach in a nice suit is unnerving at best, but when he starts telling Christine things he should not know the audience becomes confused. It is a brilliant introduction to what turns out to be a complex character and audiences go from being apprehensive about him, to hating him, and then feeling as if he vindicated himself. It is a tricky chore to pull off, but it works quite well here, which speaks volumes to the skills of the actor, script, and direction.

Alexis is simply the "coolest guy in the room." He tricks people and has a house rigged to aid him in doing so. He is also a con man targeting, it appears, rich women who do not know any better, hardly the most sympathetic victims in cinematic history, and at this period in America's history, right after World War II, there were a lot of widows to be found. Alexis is a magician and a mentalist, and his pet crow and parlor tricks are more than enough to woo any female. But never is he played in such a way that audiences think the victims deserve what they are getting, and yet we like him at the end.

Alexis' change of heart occurs when he meets Paul, who is a decidedly different kind of con artist. Alexis sees that there is a fine line between the two of them, and it is one the law will make little distinction over. Legally, Alexis is unconcerned, but morally he seems to be distraught, thinking it appalling that he would ever be lumped in with such a person, and that is what ultimately causes him to turn on the man and save the women.

Alexis' final act is to free his trained pet crow. The bird flies out the open window into the heavens on command with Alexis' soul soon to join him. Symbolically, the trickster/death/missionary is set free to be accepted by Heaven. As an audience we can feel good about Alexis' fate as we know that not only was it a sacrifice, but that he has changed his ways and will be recognized by God for that. The final scene could have been shot from above, much like the opening beach scene, as the bird leaves the room, but it is filmed from within the room instead. This gives audiences a more personal sense of closure as we are "physical" witnesses to it and not removed from the act. Alexis' redemption is not some abstract spiritual thing, as would have been indicated if shot from above. It is a personal redemption that is far more important than God's approval when it comes to the audience. That is why it is filmed in the room where a good portion of the film's action takes place. It is comfortable. It is home. The very beginning and first part of the film may have a supernatural feel to it, but by the end that has been stripped away and the events have become firmly lodged in the material world. To film the ending differently would have ruined Alexis' redemption in a way that would have harmed the film. It also made Alexis everything Christine should have been but was not.

While Alexis started out mysterious, Christine was an open book from her first scene. A rich widow living with her sister, Christine was the type of character that most films would try to make an audience feel sympathetic toward. Not here. There is a nearly constant sense of disconnect between her and the audience, and the film is better for it.

At first, Christine comes off as unapproachable. She is wealthy, widowed, and thinking of her late husband, but has a date with a man she has obviously been seeing for some time. Her indecisiveness will be a driving factor in the film, and by the time the film concludes, she will not have changed, either. It is a risky move to make a film revolve around a character whom audiences will ultimately not care all that much about and will actually become frustrated with, but it sets the film up to be something a bit unexpected. If this was done purposefully, then kudos is necessary.

As the story develops, Christine's uncertainty about the incidents in her life such as meeting Alexis, being proposed to, and thinking her late husband is coming back from the grave become more vexing as the audience is let in on the actual events that surround her. This now makes Christine come across as slightly naïve, as well. By the time her character is set to meet her doom at Paul's hands, the audience is unsympathetic to her plight. We do not want Paul to necessarily succeed in his mission to kill her, but we wish Christine would come to her senses and think that a near death incident may just be the wake-up call she needs. Unfortunately, it is not.

Christine's rescue and lack of change of heart essentially render her useless as a character from that point forward. At first this seems to be a horrible move on Vorhaus' part because Christine was the film's spine, as it were, and now that support has vanished. Instead of tanking the movie, though, it actually allows the film to reach a natural and unexpected conclusion as we finally learn that Alexis is the real focal point of the film, and it is his arc that we should have been paying attention to the entire time. In a film that is all about misdirection, this is its ace in the hole.

Another way Vorhaus keeps us on our toes is through Janet, a character who, in any other film, would cause audiences to feel about her the way they do about Christine. Instead, we sympathize with her more than her mourning, waffling sister.

Of the two sisters, Janet should not be the one we end up caring about more. She is very naïve, thinks too highly of herself, and even has an annoying voice. By the end of the film she somehow redeems herself in the viewers' eyes, and it is all done through her character's actions. Sure, she apparently falls in love with Alexis, with his help, and she believes she may have psychic powers, too, but the other things she does causes her character to develop far more fully than Christine's, and she is actually the more believable of the two.

Janet may seem to be a bit of a bother when we are first introduced to her, but that worry she displays for Christine is in character. When Janet begins to suspect that something is amiss and joins with Martin and the detective to investigate Alexis, we start to realize this is a girl who will do anything to save her sister. Falling in love with the one they are investigating is foolish, but that is also keeping in Janet's character. Going into Alexis' house as someone looking for his services, however, is not in character, but what it confirms for the audience is that she is definitely the kind of girl who is willing to go that extra step in order to help her older sibling.

Janet comes across as immature from the beginning, but it is only after we start to see all of Christine's faults that we understand the roles may really be reversed in some manner of speaking. Christine's inability to make a decision places her in a worse light than Janet's seemingly reckless abandon when it comes to decision making. It provides an interesting contrast and is just one more thing that keeps audiences feeling puzzled as the roles are a little deeper than they have come to expect in a film.

When it comes to Paul, the exact opposite is in play. There are no mixed feelings about him, but how his character is handled is done so effectively that by the time his physical body makes an appearance, audiences believe there is nothing he is incapable of doing.

Paul never comes across as a sympathetic character, though we first only know of him as corpse. From the strange song that plays on the piano, to the creepy painting, to the "voice from beyond," Paul comes across as suspect from the beginning of the film … even before we know his name. When first introduced to him through his spiritual antics, we are not aware of the direction the film is heading and think we could be watching a supernatural thriller. This makes Paul's first few appearances foreboding and steeped in the unknown. Paul, as a ghost, comes across as mildly threatening, and that is well before we know he is still alive.

In another well-choreographed bit of storytelling, once Alexis is introduced, the threat Paul represents takes a back seat to Alexis, his "powers," and potential threat level. It is nearly enough to make us forget about Paul, though his "spirit" makes a few marked appearances here and there.

Once Paul is revealed to still be alive, it is a genuine, big surprise in a movie that is full of small subtle ones. The fact that he collaborates with a hesitant Alexis, whom we also know to be corrupt at this point, shows just how nasty Paul is, and it gives us pause when it comes to Alexis.

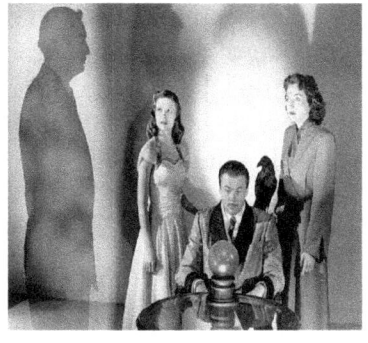

From Paul's first physical appearance to his last, he shows us that he is nothing but danger. His plot to get the sister's money and his blackmail of Alexis makes us realize we have been looking at the wrong person as a bigger threat the entire time. It is a startling revelation, and it is one that has a profound effect on the audience. While Alexis redeems himself, Paul is so corrupt and evil that such redemption is impossible. He is a murderer. He is a con artist. He is evil. And though Alexis is a con artist as well, and some may even say he is evil to prey upon the vulnerability of a widow, he is nothing compared to Paul.

This rollercoaster ride of character expectations experienced by the audience is risky to do in a film, but here it is expertly handled. Part of what makes it work so well is the understated character of Martin, who represents the audience.

Martin is the Everyman. One can imagine that he recently returned home from the war, where perhaps he was an officer, and was adjusting quite well to life in the States. His no-nonsense approach to his relationship with the widow Christine is handled very sympathetically, if not a little too much so. We understand that, though, as we realize Martin loves her and believes that if given enough time her memory of Paul will fade away. Of course, the introduction of Alexis changes things in a negative way, but Martin rides out this new development much like we imagine he does with all things, which is to say rationally and calmly.

Since we are on unsteady ground when it comes to the first half of the film, it is no surprise that Martin is our anchor to reality. His reactions and actions mirror how we feel about what is transpiring on the screen. When he is sympathetic, so are we. When he is suspicious, we follow suit. He is our able and secure guide to the film's plot . . . until Paul makes his physical appearance.

Paul's physical appearance after the séance severs our attachment to Martin so abruptly that we do not even realize it at first. All the audience knows is that everything it believed to be true no longer is, and Martin's presence does nothing to help us. We are now on our own, totally helpless to what Vorhaus has in store for us. Our guide and anchor is gone, and now we are experiencing everything from the perspective of the knowledgeable outsider who is unable to communicate with those on screen. *Halloween* (1978) did a similar thing toward its conclusion, and it is a narrative shift that works extremely well when it comes to ramping up the tension.

The characters are not the only thing that immerses the audience into Vorhaus' story. Cinematographer John Alton utilizes lighting to a masterful degree, setting the mood and keeping the audience's attention exactly where it should be. The lighting is so important that Alton wrote about it in his book, *Painting with Light* (originally published in 1949 by Macmillan Co. and reprinted in 1995 by University of California Press), which is one of the first books written by a well-established cinematographer on cinematography for cinematographers.

According to the book, Vorhaus was quoted as saying that some of the ways Alton chose to light a scene were "taboo" at the time, such as shooting right into the sun to cause glare.

Though Todd McCarthy's introduction to the book calls *The Amazing Mr. X* a "film of modest virtues," Alton references it throughout the book's two hundred plus pages through photographs which highlight the techniques he used in his various films. Reading it makes it very clear that Alton put serious thought into every shot and the mood he and Vorhaus wanted to convey to the audience. It is of no surprise that the film is featured several times throughout sections detailing "mystery" and "criminal" lighting.

While Vorhaus' overall film may be of "modest virtues," it also exceeds expectations on some levels, and part of that is due to Alton's atmospheric lighting. Alton understands that not only does lighting help emphasize aspects of the story, it also tells a story in its own right. His skill helps to sell a plot that should have been all-too-familiar to moviegoers in the late '40s, though it is done in a way that was perhaps quite unexpected.

"AND WE'D LOVE EACH OTHER THROUGH ALL ETERNITY?"

1948. World War II ended just three short years earlier, and America was adjusting to life post wartime. Widows, such as Christine, were commonplace due to servicemen being killed in combat. American society was not only adjusting to this new world where people were exposed to horrible Nazi atrocities, it was also changing in many other ways. 1948 saw *The Kinsey Report*. A year earlier the seeds were planted for the modern environmentalism movement with the publication of *The Everglades: River of Grass*. 1947 also saw the first glimpses of the modern-day UFO phenomenon manifesting in Roswell, New Mexico. Prior to that in the 1930s and 1940s, Jack Parsons made his way into the public eye, and with him came an awareness of the occult.

Parsons was a rocket scientist out of Pasadena, California and one of the founders of the Jet Propulsion Laboratory, a notch in any scientist's belt. He was also a follower of Aleister Crowley and was a member of his *Ordo Templi Orientis* lodge. Police were often called out to investigate things occurring at the lodge, though they never took the complaints too seriously.

Parsons eventually moved the lodge from Los Angeles, California to his mansion in Pasadena, where the sex magic rituals and parties continued, and attracted people like Ray Bradbury and L. Ron Hubbard.

In 1941 Alfred Ligon established the Aquarian Book Shop and Aquarian Spiritual Center in Los Angeles, both of which became a hotspot of the New Age movement, and, incidentally, the bookstore was the longest continuously owned black bookstore in the United States. Many would say it was an answer to the more nefarious goings-on of Parsons and his ilk.

America in the 1940s was dealing with a paradigm shift, of which spiritualism and the occult were a part. Fortune telling was still big business in the 1940s, as seen by fortune telling teacups one could buy, and fortune telling card decks. Americans were becoming skeptical of this activity, though, as World War II hardened the nation. The occult leanings of the Nazis may not have been well known in 1948, but people were equating the "unknown" with criminal activity on a broader level than they had been previously. The skeptical were not only outnumbering the believers, they were also becoming more prominent in the media.

In 1947 Crane Wilbur's story, *The Spiritualist*, was bought by Producers Releasing Corporation, and Wilbur was slated to direct the film version of it. Eagle Lion eventually acquired the project with the intent of making it a project for Turhan Bey, who was under contract to the film studio at the time. Vorhaus, who was now set to direct the picture, was unhappy with Wilbur's script and had it rewritten in a week. At some point in the process it was also saddled with the unfortunate title of *The Amazing Mr. X*. For Vorhaus, this was to be the first film in a two-picture deal he had signed on for with the company. It turned out to be his only film with it, however.

Upon the film's release in July of 1948, audiences throughout America apparently found many parts of the film to be unintentionally funny. Despite that, the studio was happy with the picture and offered *I Married a Communist* to Vorhaus, who turned it down. Eagle Lion then terminated his contract.

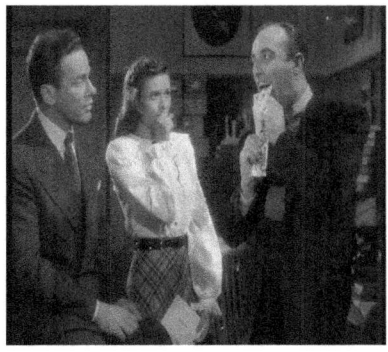

Bey, for his part, found his role to be fantastic and wished all his roles could be as interesting, though he was reportedly unhappy with his death scene.

In many ways, *The Amazing Mr. X* was both a product of its time and ahead of its time. It was obviously something special to people like Bey and Alton, and many of today's critics are also quick to point out the film's strong points and give it praise. At the time of its premiere, however, audiences had a different reaction. With the spiritualism movement under public scrutiny, the thought of a vaguely titled film dealing with that movement being a criminal enterprise seemed like it should be a surefire hit. The combined horror and *noir* aspects seemed destined for greatness, as well. Unfortunately, even the most positive current reviews put a bit of a spin on it that was also most likely common upon its release.

Edmund G. Bansak's *Fearing the Dark* (2003, McFarland & Company calls the film a "marvelously atmospheric but extremely minor 'B' quickie." Bansak goes on to write that the film is "no minor classic, but its inventiveness and visual splendor are worth some recognition."

Bansak's review mirrors nearly every other modern review of the film. Critics are quick to point out the film's faults but are also equally quick to praise its high points. It is a testament to the film that it is given such leeway when it comes to its issues.

Regardless of how critics and viewers feel about the film now, it did not have a lasting effect on audiences at the time. Nor has history dealt with it too kindly. It is not remembered like other films released in the same year, such as *Rope*, *The Naked City*, or *The Treasure of Sierra Madre*. When older, innovative horror and *noir* films are mentioned, Vorhaus' does not even merit a footnote.

Of course, it does not help that the film was cursed from the start. In fact, it almost seems quite fitting to the film itself as to how Bari came to get her starring role.

LYNN BARI

CHRISTINE FABER

Bari was born Margaret Schuyler Fisher on December 18, 1913. In 1935 she was one of 14 women who received a six-month contract with 20th Century Fox after going through the company's year-and-a-half long training program to produce actresses. She appeared in quite a few films before landing the starring role in *The Amazing Mr. X*, starting with 1933's *Meet the Baron*. From there she went on to appear in *Bottoms Up* (1934), *Charlie Chan in Paris* (1935), *Doubting Thomas* (1935), *Dante's Inferno* (1935), *Charlie Chan in Shanghai* (1935), *Professional Soldier* (1935), *The Great Ziegfeld* (1936), *City Girl* (1938), *The Return of the Cisco Kid* (1939), *Tampico* (1944), and many more. Her roles in her early films were mostly uncredited, but as the roles became more prominent, people started to take notice of her. In fact, during a World War II survey, Bari was named the second most popular pin-up girl after Betty Grable.

When it comes to *The Amazing Mr. X*, the role of Christine was not originally intended for Bari. It actually was given to Carole Landis, who signed a contract with Eagle Lion specifically for the role. Landis had become a known entity eight years earlier with 1940's *One Million B.C.*, and her nickname was

"The Chest," due to her curves. For Eagle Lion, landing Landis was a distinct win despite her rocky beginnings.

Landis, like Bari, had moved with her family to California. Bari had been in her early teens when the move occurred, and Landis was four. At 15 Landis dropped out of school to pursue 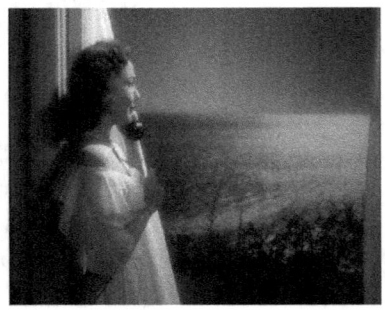 acting, though early on few seemed to think Landis would amount to anything much in show business. After appearing as an extra in *A Star is Born* (1937), posing for hundreds of cheesecake photos, and getting bit parts, she finally landed the role in *One Million B.C.* and became a star after the film was hit.

Soon after getting a contract with 20th Century Fox she began a relationship with Darryl F. Zanuck, who was its Vice President of Production. When she ended their relationship, her career faltered and she was relegated to roles in B films.

Landis' private life, meanwhile, was a whirlwind of relationships. She was married four times but had no children. Her last marriage was to W. Horace Schmidlapp, a Broadway producer, in 1945. They separated in 1947 with Landis filing for divorce in early 1948 due to "extreme mental cruelty." While separated, Landis apparently had an affair with actor Rex Harrison, who was married at the time. After

Landis' death Harrison would claim that Landis was just a close friend of the couple. Landis saw it differently.

When Harrison would not divorce his wife, Lilli Palmer, Bari overdosed on Seconal. Harrison had been the last person to see her alive the night before when they had dinner together.

The next day Harrison and Landis' maid found her body and Harrison waited several hours before calling the police. Landis had apparently left two suicide notes, one being for her mother and the other for Harrison, who denied that there had been a note for him.

Landis' family believes that Landis' death may not have been suicide. On a web page about Landis, Landis' great-niece writes that her "family never believed it was suicide. We are [one hundred percent] convinced that Rex Harrison is to blame for her death." The great-niece goes on to write that her grandmother begged the police to investigate more than they had, but they refused and then a private investigator was hired. "All he could tell her was that people were paid off and evidence destroyed."

Landis' great-niece offers a few theories on the death, noting that Harrison may have put the Seconal in Landis' food, or even that Landis took the Seconal after threatening suicide and called Harrison to save her, but he watched her die instead.

Regardless of how Landis died, she was not able to fulfill her role in Vorhaus' film and it was then offered to Bari instead.

Bari became known for playing "man killers" in her films, but *The Amazing Mr. X* casts her in a very different light. Far from being some sort of dangerous or conniving woman in the film, she is a decidedly weak character who is also far from sultry, though that is primarily due to her constant grieving and indecisiveness.

When reading about Bari one also finds an almost universal opinion regarding her talents. It seems that most people who write about her or her movies believe she should have been a bigger actress than she turned out to be in the grand scheme of Hollywood history. Bari, according to one quote attributed to her, thought that, as well. She had grown tired of being in B-movies and wanted her time to shine in something bigger.

While those roles may have never come, Bari remained far removed from the characters she played. If she was a man-killer in real life, you would not know it from reading her thoughts on her co-star Bey.

In Jeff Gordon's highly praised biography of Bari called *Foxy Lady* (BearManor Media, 2010), the actress is quoted as saying, "I liked Turhan Bey very much. People say, 'Oh, Turhan Bey,' and make fun of him. But he was a very smart guy and a real gentleman." Bari goes on to surmise that Bey's reputation as a gentleman was what killed his Hollywood career. He was too nice, according to her.

In Gordon's book Bari also admitted that she thought she would be making three films with Eagle

Lion, but instead only made two, with *The Amazing Mr. X* being the last one for the studio.

Bari's obituary in the December 1, 1989 edition of *The New York Times* had a headline that read, "Lynn Bari, 75, 'Other Woman,' in 30's and 40's Movies, is Dead." Bari may have thought she should have progressed past such roles and films, but history thought differently.

TURHAN BEY

ALEXIS

If there is one thing that is clear from Bey's performance, it is that he should have been a bigger star.

Born in 1922 and dying in 2012, Bey was known by his fans as the "Turkish Delight" due to his Turkish origin. His first major acting role came in 1941's *Shadows on the Stairs*. He has also appeared in *Raiders of the Desert* (1941); *The Gay Falcon* (1941); *Drums of the Congo* (1942); *Destination Unknown* (1942); *The Mummy's Tomb* (1942); *Arabian Nights* (1942); *White Savage* (1943); *The Mad Ghoul* (1943); *Ali Baba and the Forty Thieves* (1944); *Prisoners of the Casbah* (1953); and various TV series including *SeaQuest 2032*; *Murder, She Wrote*; and *Babylon 5*.

Bey was an acting success story straight out of a Hollywood movie. According to a May 19, 1945 article titled "Czech Boy Makes Good" in the Australian newspaper the *Voice*, Bey, at the time 23 years old, gave performances that were "precise, etched with poise, sophistication and cultured menace." The article, written by Tas Hobart, goes on to state that when Bey came to America "he could only speak enough English to order a meal." It also credited his career in film to his pursuit to learn English.

When Bey and his mother arrived in America, Bey wanted to study English so he enrolled in Ben Bard's School of Dramatic Arts. One of the courses he took was Dramatics and "[e]ight months after he enrolled in the school he was playing the lead role . . . in a psychological drama staged by Bard."

Bey loved playing the "weird" character in what the actor called a "mystical kind of a drama." From there, after about the third night of the play, Warner Bros. called Bey and offered him a role in a movie with Errol Flynn. The movie was *Footsteps in the Dark* (1941).

In a 1995 interview between Skip E. Lowe and Bey, which can be found on Youtube, Bey recounted his early Hollywood memories, and came across as nothing but a gentleman.

At the time of the interview, Bey lived in Vienna, and spent his days taking photographs of nature and "young ladies." Bey also talked of his morning routine, which involved waking up at five a.m., taking a cold shower, not drying off, going back to bed wet, and covering up and being dry a half hour later. He called it an "old German method" of remaining young.

Oddly enough, Lowe takes great delight in telling Bey that he discovered that Bey's autographed photo is worth a paltry thirty-five dollars. Bey handled the news very humbly, stating that it was more than what some of his co-stars' pictures were worth despite them working harder than himself

When asked if there were anything he would change in his life if he could go back in time, he said he would be more professional when it came to his acting.

According to the October 10, 2012 obituary in *The Guardian*, Bey wished to marry Lana Turner in 1944, but broke off their relationship because his mother, to whom he was very close, disapproved. Bey continued to think highly of Turner, however, mentioning her repeatedly in Lowe's interview, and apparently still trying to get her roles in films, as *Billboard* reported in its November 22, 1947 edition where the publication reported a bit of gossip that Bey was trying to get Turner to replace another actor on a film.

When it comes to *The Amazing Mr. X*, Thomas M. Feramisco's book *The Mummy Unwrapped: Scenes Left on Universal's Cutting Room Floor* (McFarland & Company, 2007) reveals that Bey felt his performance in the film could have been "stronger." What is obvious to anyone watching the film, however, is not only is his performance strong, it also saved the film.

CATHY O'DONNELL

JANET

O'Donnell was born Ann Steely in July of 1923 (though some sources report the year as 1925). Her story is another classic Hollywood tale. She was actually studying acting at Oklahoma City University and saving money for a two-week trip to Hollywood to try her hand at acting. During that trip she was spotted by a talent agent who brought her to Samuel Goldwyn, who signed her to a contract. One of the first things she needed to do, however, was change her name.

According to William Hare's *L.A. Noir: Nine Dark Visions of the City of Angels* (McFarland & Company 2008), she picked the name Cathy after the *Wuthering Heights* character. It was Mrs. Frances Goldwyn who suggested O'Donnell because "the public loves Irish names."

O'Donnell's first film role was as an extra in 1945's *Wonder Man*. A year later she appeared in *The Best Years of Our Lives* with roles in other movies and later in television following. Some of her movies and shows include *Bury Me Dead* (1947), *They Live by Night* (1948), *Never Trust a Gambler* (1951), the underrated *Lights Out* TV series, *Mad at the World* (1955), *The Deerslayer* (1957), *My World Dies Screaming* (1958), the TV series *Target*, and her final movie being the classic *Ben-Hur* (1959). The early part of the Sixties found her only appearing in various television series, including a 1964 episode of *Bonanza*, which was her final acting role.

When O'Donnell was 24 she married Robert Wyler, who was 47 at the time. They remained married, and she died on her 22nd wedding anniversary, with him passing away nine months later. Her story was yet another from this film's cast that was truly made for Hollywood.

RICHARD CARLSON

MARTIN

Carlson, born in 1912, is one of those actors who appeared in many films and television shows, but never quite became a huge star.

Inarguably, the most famous film Carlson was in was 1954's *Creature from the Black Lagoon*. He appeared in many other films before and after that, however, and also served as a director for television and movies, as well as a writer for television.

His first role, which was uncredited, was 1935's *Desert Death*. Other films he appeared in included *Winter Carnival* (1939), *The Ghost Breakers* (1940), *West Point Widow* (1941), *The Affairs of Martha* (1942), *A Stranger in Town* (1943), *King Solomon's Mines* (1950), and *It Came from Outer Space* (1953). His final film role, which was voice work, was for the 1974 short film *Freedom 2000*.

He was also in many television series, including *Lights Out*, like his co-star O'Donnell. He also appeared in *Lancer*, *The F.B.I.*, *Perry Mason*, *I Led 3 Lives*, and many, many more.

Carlson died in 1977. In his *New York Times* obituary, dated November 27, 1977, there was a quote that Carlson gave an interviewer in 1959 when the subject of him transitioning from movies to television came up.

"I have little patience," Carlson said, "with people who think that the money television pays is tainted. I love money. The more of it, the better. I want prosperity for my family, and television gives it to me."

The obituary also quotes Carlson regarding his roles in the movies. "I was the guy who did not get the girl. I was not going any higher."

DONALD CURTIS

PAUL

Curtis, as one look at his IMDB.com page would show, was a busy man. Born in 1915, this one-time pastor appeared in over 100 movies and television shows. These include *Junior G-Men* (1940), *Today I Hang* (1942), *National Velvet* (1944), *It Came From Beneath the Sea* (1955), *Earth vs. the Flying Saucers* (1956), *The Ten Commandments* (1956), and many more. Some of the television shows he appeared in include the classics like *The Beverly Hillbillies*, *My Three Sons*, *Science Fiction Theatre*, *Green Acres*, and more.

The *Chicago Tribune* ran a piece on Curtis in its July 7, 1946 edition titled "Don Curtis, Ex-Professor." Writer Freida Zylstra wrote that Curtis was one of the few college professors to become an actor in Hollywood. The article gave a overview of Curtis' non-Hollywood lifestyle, pointing out his love of gardening and how he was an expert horseman and swimmer who liked to play squash. The photos accompanying the article focused on him and his young daughter doing various at-home activities. Readers may have been surprised to learn that just two years later he would be playing a sinister murderer and blackmailer.

BERNARD VORHAUS

DIRECTOR

Director Vorhaus was born on Christmas 1904 in New York City. His first work in Hollywood was as a screenwriter in his twenties, but like many of his screenwriter peers, he wanted to direct. This desire led him to go to England where he got his chance to direct and became successful enough to come back to America and start directing films for Republic Pictures.

Some of Vorhaus' work as a director includes *The Singing City* (1930), *Crime on the Hill* (1933), *The Ghost Camera* (1933), *Dark World* (1935), *Fisherman's Wharf* (1939), *Angels with Broken Wings* (1941), *Bury Me Dead* (1947), and *So Young, So Bad* (1950).

Vorhaus, also like many of his Hollywood peers, was blacklisted by the House of Unamerican Activities. This was in 1951, when Vorhaus had already moved back to Europe. Eventually he stayed in England, retired from film altogether, and founded a business that specialized in renovating houses.

Vorhaus had two children, one of whom was David Vorhaus, who became an electronic music pioneer and performed as White Noise, a seminal electronic music act that influenced, and some would say created, the entire genre of that style of music.

Vorhaus passed away in 2000, seemingly forgotten in the film world.

"DOES THIS FEEL ... UNCOMFORTABLE TO YOU?"

Mixing *noir* and the paranormal effectively is not an easy feat, but *The Amazing Mr. X* makes it look that way. It is also a film that is as surprising as it is disappointing in many ways. As good as it is, the viewer cannot help wanting it to be better.

What makes this film stand out among other *noir* and horror films is that it straddles the line between both genres in the beginning in a way that is sophisticated and keenly aware of audience expectations.

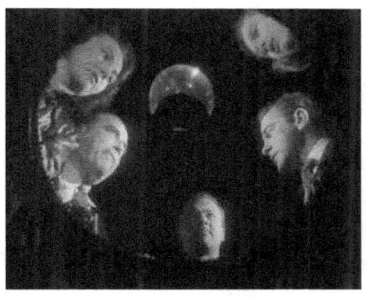

It plays with all the expectations of those genres and then delivers what is ultimately a standard *noir* crime drama. It is believable for the most part, and it is entertaining enough to keep its issues from getting in the way of the story, but that desire for it to really rise above its station is strong throughout, and for a film buff that is what leads to disappointment.

In many ways, this film is also ahead of its time as much as it is a product of it. Its teasing of the audience and use of light were well ahead of what the majority of other films were doing in the late 1940s. If it had been a bigger, more popular film, it most likely would have had a lasting impact upon American cinema. It would have been heavily cited by film historians, and it would have been considered by many to be a classic. Unfortunately, it was a film dominated by mid-level stars and directed by a man who was never destined to be a household name. Had this concept come to light just a few years later, however, it probably would have never been made as both *noir* and spiritualism weakened on the public's radar. Luck and craftsmanship were on its side as far as film history goes, but a standard, fairly clichéd plot and a cast and crew who never really rose above their lot in cinematic life hampered it just as much. Rarely do you see a film from this period straddle that line as well as this one does, and that is part of the reason it deserves some attention.

The Amazing Mr. X is a little-known cultural artifact of curiosity and wonder. It speaks volumes of an era that has passed us by. The movie exemplifies audiences' desires to see crime and horror played out on the screen, but also be paid for by the end credits. The story details the desperation of the naïve privileged people who are trying to connect with things they cannot buy with the money they possess just as well as it details the greed of those who were not lucky enough to have come into wealth, but so desperately crave it that they will murder for it. The actual finished product showcases what can be done with ingenuity, skill, and hope, and proves one does not have to be a marquee star to turn in a star-worthy performance.

If one looks into the online reviews, written by the average viewer, you will notice a trend toward the positive, with many people stating what a gem of a film it is. These reviews all come decades after the film's initial release, which is telling. Many films from the 1940s have a hard time keeping a modern audience's interest, with the common complaints being that there is too much dialogue and not enough action. Those complaints do not find their way to this film. If anything, it seems like the modern audience has decided that this film is worth watching despite not having all the bells and whistles of today's mainstream features.

Unfortunately, the film's current positive reviews cannot change its past performance. According to the-numbers.com, the highest grossing films of 1948 were *The Snake Pit*, *Red River*, and *Key Largo*, with *The Snake Pit* grossing $10 million. Impressive for 1948. Tellingly, *The Amazing Mr. X* was not even in the top 12 highest grossing films for that year.

Currently, not everyone finds the film to their liking, either. Michael Weldon's *Psychotronic Encyclopedia of Film* (Ballantine Books, 1983) reviews it under its other title of *The Spiritualist* (and also erroneously lists the film as *The Amazing Dr. X*) finds the film derivative of *Nightmare Alley* (1947). And that is all Weldon has to say about it other than a brief bit on the plot.

Weldon *and* the viewers who love it are both correct. It is an overall competent film with some great moments and scenes. It is also derivative and clichéd. It came at a time when America was still getting over WWII and spiritualism was being met with more skepticism than in the past. If Alexis' character had not redeemed himself at the end, it is unlikely anyone would care for this film despite its excellent lighting and how the film started out tweaking the cinematic story conventions audiences were used to at the time. That unconventional plot started out fine, but by the end of the film it became just another *noir* thriller, albeit with a likable villain who turned out to be not so bad after all. Moviegoers then had seen this sort of thing. Today's audiences, with Weldon naturally being an exception as he has watched plenty of *noir*, are not used to the tropes of the genre, and that is part of the reason they have embraced this film.

Far too many movies get worse with age. Some remain timeless. It is rare when one actually becomes better as time goes on. The *Amazing Mr. X* is that rarity. Too bad the principle players in it are not around to see its positive reviews.

Index

20th Century Fox, 33, 34
A Star is Born, 34
A Stranger in Town, 45
Affairs of Martha, The, 45
Ali Baba and the Forty Thieves, 39
Alton, John, 27, 28, 31
Amazing Dr. X, The, 53
Amazing Mr. X, The, iii, 15, 17, 27, 31, 33, 36, 37, 41, 51, 52, 53, 54
anarchist, 16
Angels with Broken Wings, 49
Aquarian Book Shop, 30
Aquarian Spiritual Center, 30
Arabian Nights, 39
Babylon 5, 39
Ballantine Books, 53
Bansak, Edmund G., 32
Bard, Ben, 40
Bari, Lynn, 5, 32, 33, 34, 35, 36, 37
BearManor Media, 36
Ben Bard's School of Dramatic Arts, 40
Ben-Hur, 44
Best Years of Our Lives, The, 43
Beverly Hillbillies, The, 47
Bey, Turhan, 6, 30, 31, 36, 39, 40, 41
Billboard, 41
Blast, The, 16
Bonanza, 44
Bottoms Up, 33
Bradbury, Ray, 30
Bury Me Dead, 43, 49
Carlson, Richard, 5, 45, 46
Charlie Chan in Paris, 33
Charlie Chan in Shanghai, 33
Chicago Tribune, 47
City Girl, 33
Creature from the Black Lagoon, 45
Crime on the Hill, 49
Crowley, Aleister, 29
Curtis, Donald, 5, 47
Dante's Inferno, 33
Dark World, 49
Deerslayer, The, 43
Desert Death, 45
Destination Unknown, 39
Doubting Thomas, 33
Drums of the Congo, 39
Eagle Lion, 30, 31, 33, 37
Earth vs. the Flying Saucers, 47
England, 49
Europe, 49
Everglades: River of Grass, The, 29
F.B.I., The, 45
Fearing the Dark, 32
Feramisco, Thomas M., 41
Fisher, Margaret Schuyler, 33
Fisherman's Wharf, 49
Flynn, Errol, 40
Footsteps in the Dark, 40

Foxy Lady, 36
Freedom 2000, 45
Gay Falcon, The, 39
Ghost Breakers, The, 45
Ghost Camera, The, 49
Goldwyn, Frances, 43
Goldwyn, Samuel, 43
Gordon, Jeff, 36, 65
Grable, Betty, 33
Great Ziegfeld, The, 33
Green Acres, 47
Gregg, Virginia, 6
Guardian, The, 41
Halloween, 27
Hare, William, 43
Harrison, Rex, 34, 35
Hobart, Tas, 39
Hollywood, 36, 39, 40, 43, 44, 47, 49, 64
House of Unamerican Activities, 49
Hubbard, L. Ron, 30
I Led 3 Lives, 45
I Married a Communist, 31
It Came From Beneath the Sea, 47
It Came from Outer Space, 45
Jet Propulsion Laboratory, 29
Julius, Emanuel, 16
Junior G-Men, 47
Key Largo, 53
King Solomon's Mines, 45
Kinsey Report, The, 29
Lancer, 45
Landis, Carole, 33, 34, 35
Lights Out, 43, 45
Ligon, Alfred, 30
Los Angeles, California, 29, 30
Lowe, Skip E., 40, 41
Macmillan Co., 27
Mad at the World, 43

Mad Ghoul, The, 39
McCarthy, Todd, 27
McFarland & Company, 32, 41, 43
Meet the Baron, 33
Mendoza, Harry, 9
Mummy Unwrapped: Scenes Left on Universal's Cutting Room Floor, The, 41
Mummy's Tomb, The, 39
Murder, She Wrote, 39
My Three Sons, 47
My World Dies Screaming, 43
Naked City, The, 32
National Velvet, 47
Nazis, 30
Never Trust a Gambler, 43
New York City, 49
New York Times, The, 37, 45
Nightmare Alley, 53
O'Donnell, Cathy, 5, 43, 44, 45
Oklahoma City University, 43
One Million B.C., 33, 34
Ordo Templi Orientis, 29
Painting with Light, 27
Palmer, Lilli, 35
Parsons, Jack, 29, 30
Pasadena, California, 29
Perry Mason, 45
Prisoners of the Casbah, 39
Producers Releasing Corporation, 30
Professional Soldier, 33
Psychotronic Encyclopedia of Film, 53
Raiders of the Desert, 39
Red River, 53
Republic Pictures, 49
Return of the Cisco Kid, The, 33
Rope, 32

Roswell, New Mexico, 29
San Francisco, 16
Schmidlapp, W. Horace, 34
Science Fiction Theatre, 47
SeaQuest 2032, 39
Seconal, 35
Shadows on the Stairs, 39
Singing City, The, 49
Snake Pit, The, 53
So Young, So Bad, 49
Spiritualist, The, 16, 53; Story, 30
Steely, Ann, 43
Strange Mr. X, The, 16
Tampico, 33
Target, 43
Ten Commandments, The, 47
the-numbers.com, 53
They Live by Night, 43
Today I Hang, 47
Treasure of Sierra Madre, The, 32
Turkish Delight, 39
Turner, Lana, 41

University of California Press, 27
Vienna, 40
Voice, 39
Vorhaus, Bernard, 17, 18, 22, 23, 26, 27, 28, 30, 31, 32, 35, 49, 50
Vorhaus, David, 49
Warner Bros., 40
Weldon, Michael, 53, 54
West Point Widow, 45
White Noise, 49
White Savage, 39
Wilbur, Crane, 30
Winter Carnival, 45
Wonder Man, 43
World War II, 20, 29, 30, 33
Wuthering Heights, 43
WWII. *See* World War II
Wyler, Robert, 44
Youtube, 40
Zanuck, Darryl F., 34
Zylstra, Freida, 47

Doug Brunell is the author of the critically-acclaimed novels *Nothing Men* and *Black Devil Spine*. His interests include film, rare books and monitoring earthquakes for occult activity. He currently resides in Northern California with his daughter and is at work on his next novel, which will continue to push horror to its limits.

Other Works by Doug Brunell

Sinful Cinema Series

The Abductors-Nubile young cheerleaders! Sex slavers! Nudity! Bondage! Guns! Kidnapping! Torture! Sexual assault! Disney!

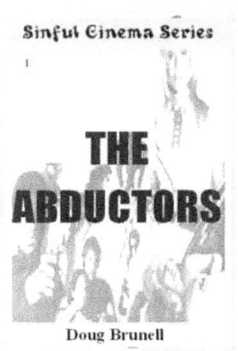

Plus: Anti-abortion terrorism, prostitutes, an infamous porn star, and an exclusive interview with Jeramie Rain (*The Last House on the Left*)!

This is a critical look at the 1972 grindhouse movie *The Abductors*, which helped set the standard for the strong female "secret agent" film while at the same time being described as "sexist" and "anti-PC." Prepare yourself for a sleazy descent into the world of sexploitation, real-life terrorism and, yes, Disney. You may think you know the movie, but you'll never view it the same way again after reading this.

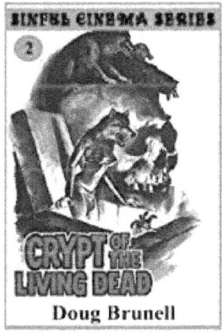

Crypt of the Living Dead-In 1973 the world was introduced to a film that was quite unlike any vampire movie before or since. While it acknowledged the legend of the bloodsucker and teased at the occult, it also wanted very little to do with either, making for a cinematic experience as confusing as it was captivating. Adding to its allure was a star who was the main suspect in a bizarre murder case that had ties to psychics and the JFK assassination, and a co-star who went on to produce some of Hollywood's most critically acclaimed and beloved films. This is . . . *Crypt of the Living Dead*!

Destruction Kings-Inspired by *Bad Boys* and *The Monster Squad*, the hilarious and offensive *Destruction Kings* caused the director to have panic attacks, divided audiences, and starred a man in an ape mask and a white guy in a Don King wig. And let's not forget John Stamos and Bill Cosby! This examination of the film also includes exclusive interviews with director/star/writer Chris Seaver, Ariauna Albright, and several others. Prepare to be amazed . . .

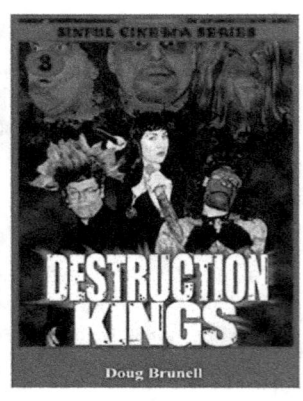

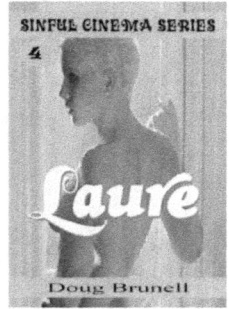

Laure-It was to be the motion picture that captured the public's attention much the same way the *Emmanuelle* film had done, and it would do so by being written and directed by the author of the *Emmanuelle* novel. What moviegoers received, however, was a film directed by a French diplomat "sex maniac" who hid his identity from the world as he preached his sexual philosophy. This is the story of *Laure*, an erotic cinematic adventure of distinct and taboo pleasures, deceit, and an initial leading lady (Linda Lovelace) who refused to do nude scenes.

Novels

Nothing Men-For years there have been rumors of inhuman things inhabiting the forests and mountains that make up the Trinity Alps of Northern California. Bigfoot. UFOs. Ghosts. Vampires. One family is about to learn the truth about these rumors as their summer vacation quickly turns into a one-way trip to Hell. No one is safe and nothing is sacred when dealing with the Nothing Men. Available in paperback and for eReaders.

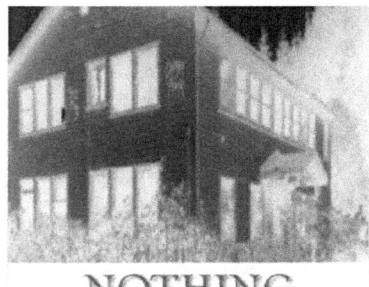
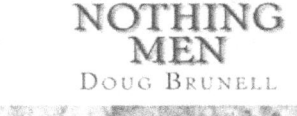

Nothing Men made me think about the likes of Herschell Gordon Lewis, Tobe Hooper, and prompted flashbacks of films like *The Wicker Man* and [the] *Texas Chainsaw Massacre*. --cinema-crazed.com

Fighting my gag reflex, I can say that I really enjoyed this book. It's not something I would ever recommend to, say, my mom, or, like, my fellow PTA members, but for those of you who like a straight-up hardcore horror story, you will find a lot to like here. -- thehorrorhoneys.com

When *NOTHING MEN*, an independently published novel, landed in my lap, I was unsure what to expect. A blurb that hinted at the supernatural and paranormal immediately grabbed my attention and as a horror fan, I felt confident that the book would have an interesting story to tell that I hoped I would enjoy. Fortunately, I was right, but nothing could prepare me for the trip I was about to take . . . -- Horrorcultfilms.com

Black Devil Spine-Dan Gere is a bestselling author in desperate need of another book idea. When he meets Martin Springer, a reclusive painter and fetish photographer, it seems he has discovered the solution to his problem. What follows, however, is a sickening descent into insanity, sexual violence and depravity like few have ever witnessed. Erotophonophilia, autassassinophilia, biastophilia-a deadly trio of paraphilias where normality does not apply and desire is synonymous with death. Some victims are more willing than others . . .

Doug Brunell isn't worried about limits or steering clear of uncharted taboo. *Black Devil Spine* is the most intense and graphic horror novel you will ever read. -- Zisi Emporium for B Movies

Black Devil Spine is a novel of graphic horror ... it deals with sexual violence without watering it down or romanticizing it . . . would recommend this book if you enjoy books such as *The Silence of the Lambs* by Thomas Harris. -- Bleedingcool.com

Doug Brunell is back with his most traumatic work yet . . . *Black Devil Spine* is the most frightening thing I've ever read and puts even the most violent horror movie to shame . . . This is a horror novel like no other

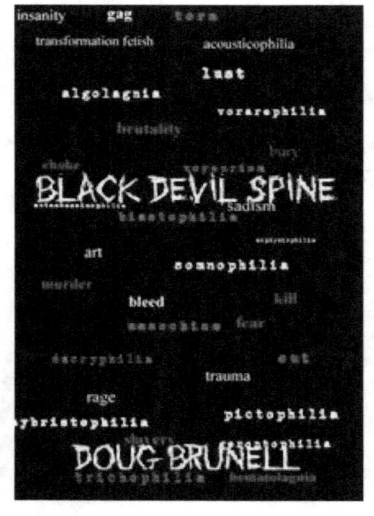

and is a journey of discovery to the darkest depths of the depraved soul rather than a novel that can be 'enjoyed' in the traditional sense. You have been warned! -- HorrorCultFilms.com

Reading this book is much like placing oneself in a carnival ride. From its description alone, you know you're in for a wild ride. However, as the ride reaches its apex the realization hits that this isn't the safest place to be . . . [A]s the latch [closes], the only thing holding you to your seat, lifts to your horror you cling on tighter. As it slides then plummets from your sweaty grasp you frantically search, cling onto anything to keep you from slipping into the abyss. A destination that when reached is assured to change your life forever . . . *Black Devil Spine* is much like that. It reads at a rollicking pace, widens the eyes with human based atrocity (universes apart from those covered in any *Shades of Grey* novel) and shatters preconceived notions of how the storyline should develop based on texts experienced before it. --Drunkinagraveyard.com

Short Stories

A Dead Friend-An off-the-cuff remark at a sleep overturns three boys' lives upside down when they learn why it isn't always a good idea to disturb the dead. Available for eReaders.

Melinda-When the homeless girl Raven accepts an offer of $5,000 to live with Travis temporarily, she has no idea that the grandfatherly widower has a very nasty surprise waiting for her. What starts as a strange, but kind offer ends in one of the most twisted ways imaginable. And he isn't through yet ... Available for eReaders.

Calling the Dead-Larson Fastings, investigative reporter, is intrigued by the man he's been watching stare out the window of his apartment for two weeks straight. When curiosity gets the best of him and he decides to question the stranger, he quickly finds himself in over his head with a man whose cruelty knows few limits. The Amazon Shorts hit is available again for the first time in over ten years! Available for eReaders.

The Good Doctor Ambrose-The folks of Dunsbrook are a simple, fearful people who have embraced a strange cult, but their doctor harbors no such delusions. He is a man of science, after all. When a child is born of a villager's tryst with an outsider, it is up to the Good Doctor Ambrose to show the townspeople that the child is free of demon blood. What they are about to find out, however, is that their doctor may have a few dark secrets of his own. Available for eReaders.

Abeunt Studia in Mores-Practice becomes habit. Habit becomes compulsion. Compulsion becomes obsession. Obsession becomes you. Available for eReaders.

Candy-Nate Helton needed a break, and the cabin he inherited in the forests of the Poconos was the perfect place to get away. Those woods hold a wonderful, magical secret, however, and Nate is about to be one of the privileged few to be let in on it. Unfortunately for him, some secrets are best left unlearned, especially when it comes to Candy. Available for eReaders.

The Power of Positive Visual Thinking-Keep telling yourself how important you are. Keep visualizing who and what you want to be. Envision your destiny. Become who you are meant to be. Embrace all that is great about you. Become the killer you know lurks inside you. Available for eReaders.

The Atrocity Channel-The Gabriel Satellite Dishmaster is 1997's premier satellite television experience. Over 200 channels of premium adult, news, sports, science-fiction, horror, foreign language and religious programming. Many of it is exclusive to Gabriel. We guarantee you've never seen anything like it. Become one of the elite. Become one of the enlightened. Become a Gabriel subscriber. It will change your life. (Certain groups need not apply.) Available for eReaders.

Night Fishing-If there is one thing Billy and Clemmy look forward to, it's night fishing. There's nothing more relaxing than eating their catch under the stars without their wives there to nag them. Tonight they are heading to their favorite fishing hole . . . and their lives will never be the same. Available for eReaders.

The Last Night of the Talk Show-Martin Randall and his wife had big plans for when his show went off the air. Unfortunately, she did not live long enough to see that happen, and now the aging former host has to face a life spent alone. But when he goes back to the place he and his deceased wife used to visit, a young couple shows him that maybe he can recapture the lost spark of his youth. Real life, however, sometimes gets in the way . . . Available for eReaders.

The Devil is a Notion-Mark Arnold is on top of the world. He promoted to his current position fast, and believes he's going to promote up even quicker. Unfortunately, Mark is also a very nasty boss, and his employees are about to show him what happens when you push people a little too far. Available for eReaders.

A Quiet House-One man whose family has gone away for a few weeks is about to discover that sometimes the worst thing one can be is alone. Alone in a quiet house that isn't so quiet anymore . . . Available for eReaders.

A Fine Summer Day in Humboldt- Tim and Laura wanted nothing more on their Humboldt vacation than to eat at nice restaurants and hike underneath the legendary redwood trees. Unfortunately, a group of tree worshipers has something else in mind for them, making it a vacation they will never forget. A folk horror tale from deep in the forests of Humboldt County, California. Available for eReaders.

www.ingramcontent.com/pod-product-compliance
Lightning Source LLC
Chambersburg PA
CBHW071752240526
45465CB00031B/691